When Jesus was young

Story by Penny Frank

Illustrated by John Haysom

THE LION
STORY BIBLE

33

OXFORD · BATAVIA · SYDNEY

The Bible tells us how God sent his Son Jesus to show us what God is like and how we can belong to God's kingdom.

This is the story of what happened after the baby Jesus was born in Bethlehem.

You can find this story in your own Bible, in Matthew's Gospel, chapter 2, and Luke's Gospel, chapter 2.

Copyright © 1986 Lion Publishing

Published by
Lion Publishing plc
Sandy Lane West, Littlemore, Oxford, England
ISBN 0 85648 758 9
Lion Publishing Corporation
1705 Hubbard Avenue, Batavia,
Illinois 60510, USA
ISBN 0 85648 758 9
Albatross Books Pty Ltd
PO Box 320, Sutherland, NSW 2232, Australia
ISBN 0 86760 542 1

First edition 1986
Reprinted 1987, 1988

Printed in Yugoslavia
Bound in Great Britain

British Library Cataloguing in Publication Data

Frank, Penny
  When Jesus was young. - (The Lion Story Bible; v33)
  1. Jesus Christ - Childhood - Juvenile literature 2. Bible stories, English - N.T.
  I. Title   II. Haysom, John
232.9'2   BT320

ISBN 0-85648-758-9

Library of Congress Cataloging in Publication Data

Frank, Penny.
When Jesus was young.
(The Lion Story Bible: 33)
1. Jesus Christ — Childhood — Juvenile literature. [1. Jesus Christ — Childhood.
2. Bible stories — N.T.] I. Haysom, John, ill. II. Title. III. Series: Frank, Penny.
Lion Story Bible; 33.
BT320.F73 1986   232.9'2
85-23866
ISBN 0-85648-758-9

Wise men from a far-off land had come
to see Jesus when he was born in
Bethlehem. They had seen a bright star
in the sky. It meant that a great new
king had been born. And so they set out
to bring him their special presents.

But the star did not lead them straight to Bethlehem. When they reached the city of Jerusalem it seemed to stop.

The wise men went at once to King Herod's palace.

'That's where the new prince will be,' they said.

King Herod was not pleased to hear about a new king.

'There is no baby king here,' he said. He sent for his advisers.

'The King God promised will be born in Bethlehem,' they told him.

So King Herod sent the wise men on their way.

'When you find him, come and tell me,' he said. He was a cruel man and had made a wicked plan.

The wise men found Jesus and gave him
their presents, but they did not go back
to King Herod. God sent them a
warning.

'Don't tell the king where Jesus is,' he
said. 'Go home another way.'

The king waited a long time for them. At last he gave up and called his soldiers.

'Go to Bethlehem,' he told them, 'and get rid of every baby boy. I don't want any new king growing up. Not one of them must be left alive.'

The soldiers set off at once.

But before they reached Bethlehem, God gave Joseph a special message.

'You must take my Son away,' he said. 'If you stay in Bethlehem King Herod will kill him.'

So Joseph and Mary packed quickly and took the baby Jesus to Egypt. King Herod could not hurt him there.

They were sad to leave their own land. They did not know how long they would be away.

But King Herod was old and ill. After a short time, he died. God told Joseph that it was safe at last for them to take Jesus home to Nazareth. Mary and Joseph were very excited.

Their friends in Nazareth ran to meet them. It was the first time they had seen Jesus.

'What a good-looking boy Mary and Joseph have,' they said. 'How big he is.'

Joseph and Mary smiled. They were so happy to be home.

14

Joseph started to work as a carpenter again. He made wooden tables and benches and tools for the farmers.

The people said, 'We are glad you have come home. You are such a good carpenter. We have missed you.'

As Jesus grew up, he watched Joseph, busy in his workshop. He played with the curly wood-shavings. Soon he was learning how to use the carpenter's tools.

Once a week, on Saturday, everyone had
a rest from work. They went to the
synagogue to pray and to hear God's
Law. It was read out loud from long
scrolls.

16

When they were six, the boys went to
school in the synagogue on weekdays.
The teacher helped them to learn God's
Law by heart and he explained it to
them. Jesus went with the others. He
remembered his lessons well.

Soon Jesus was twelve. On his thirteenth birthday, after a special service in the synagogue, he and the other boys would be treated as grown-ups.

Every year Mary and Joseph, with a
great crowd of people from Nazareth,
went to Jerusalem for the special
Passover Festival.

They walked all the way, camping out
at night. This year, for the first time,
Jesus went with Mary and Joseph.

They all had a wonderful time in Jerusalem. Each day they went to the temple to hear the teachers and to worship God. On Passover night there was a special meal. They remembered how God had rescued his people, long ago, when they were slaves in Egypt.

20

Jesus did not stay with Mary and Joseph all the time. He went with his friends. That was how they lost him on the way home.

When everyone camped for the night, Joseph and Mary could not find Jesus. No one had seen him all day. They would have to go back to Jerusalem to look for him.

It took them all day to get there. Next
morning, Joseph and Mary found Jesus
in the temple, talking to the teachers.
Mary was very annoyed with him.

'Didn't you know we'd be worried?'
she said.

'Surely you knew I'd be here, in my real Father's house,' Jesus answered. 'I must learn what he wants me to do.'

Then Joseph and Mary understood. Jesus knew he was God's Son. He was growing up. Soon he would have special work to do.

The Lion Story Bible is made up of 52 individual stories for young readers, building up an understanding of the Bible as one story — God's story — a story for all time and all people.

The New Testament section (numbers 31–52) covers the life and teaching of God's Son, Jesus. The stories are about the people he met, what he did and what he said. Almost all we know about the life of Jesus is recorded in the four Gospels — Matthew, Mark, Luke and John. The word gospel means 'good news'.

The last four stories in this section are about the first Christians, who started to tell others the 'good news', as Jesus had commanded them — a story which continues today all over the world.

The stories in *When Jesus was young* come from the New Testament. The visit of the wise men is from Matthew's Gospel, chapter 2; Jesus in Jerusalem from Luke's Gospel, chapter 2, verses 41–52. Almost nothing is known of the years between.

Mary and Joseph had not forgotten God's message through the angel, before he was born, or the strange events at the time of his birth. But the visit to Jerusalem reminded them again that Jesus was God's Son, sent into our world for a very special purpose. And Jesus, as he grew, was beginning to discover for himself what God his Father wanted him to do.

The next book in the series, number 34: *Jesus' special friends*, tells what happened when Jesus was grown-up.